WINDSOR CASTLE

Thank you to everyone who has been involved in convening communities, families, neighbours and friends to mark my Platinum Jubilee, in the United Kingdom and across the Commonwealth. I know that many happy memories will be created at these festive occasions.

I continue to be inspired by the goodwill shown to me, and hope that the coming days will provide an opportunity to reflect on all that has been achieved during the last seventy years, as we look to the future with confidence and enthusiasm.

I send my warm good wishes to you all.

Elizabeth R

CLARENCE HOUSE

In celebrating the Platinum Jubilee, we are taking part in a truly historic moment.

In 2022, Her Majesty The Queen will have reigned for seventy years. Never before has a British monarch reigned for so long.

Across the country and around the world, Platinum Jubilee parties, parades and processions are taking place as people express their admiration and appreciation for Her Majesty.

In 1947, on her twenty-first birthday, The Queen made a pledge to serve her country and the Commonwealth for her entire life. She has honoured that vow ever since through many decades of serving communities across the United Kingdom and the Commonwealth. Every passing day proves that commitment more fully, and deepens the respect we feel in turn.

As a small boy of four, I was present when my mother was crowned in 1953. Over the years since then, I have witnessed The Queen's enduring devotion to duty, her unfailing strength in times of sorrow, her unstinting generosity of spirit and her constant faith in humanity.

Through all this, my mother was sustained by her faith, by her husband and family and by the support of the people to whose welfare she has dedicated her life of exemplary service. Such devotion to the wellbeing of others is central to the values and ideals which we share as a society and, as we celebrate this Jubilee, we affirm those values too.

Together with my family, I join you all in wishing my mother, The Queen, the most marvellous Jubilee, and thank her for seventy years of unprecedented service. I am enormously proud to be sharing the Jubilee with all of you and hope you treasure this commemorative publication as your own souvenir of this very special time.

CONTENTS

A Message from Her Majesty The Queen	3
A Message from His Royal Highness The Prince of Wales	5
Introduction	10

The Platinum Jubilee Weekend

Trooping the Colour	12
Platinum Jubilee Beacons	16
Service of Thanksgiving	18
The Epsom Derby	20
Platinum Party at the Palace	22
Big Platinum Jubilee Lunch	26
Platinum Pudding Competition	28
Platinum Jubilee Pageant	32

Platinum Jubilee at the Royal Residences *Three Jubilee displays to visit*	34
The Queen's Reign *The story of her seven decades*	42
Jubilees Past and Present *Charting Royal Jubilees from 1935 to the present*	58
Seven Decades of Royal Style *Focus on Her Majesty's impeccable style*	60
The Platinum Queen *A look at the Crown Jewels & The Queen's own collection*	69
The Queen's Green Canopy *Plant a Tree for the Jubilee*	74
A Gallop Through History *Hosted by the Royal Windsor Horse Show*	80

PUBLICATIONS UK

The Official Souvenir Programme of Her Majesty The Queen's Platinum Jubilee is published by Publications UK for and on behalf of the Royal Household. Telephone: +44 (0)20 8238 5023. Website: *www.publicationsuk.co.uk*

EDITOR	PUBLISHER & MANAGING DIRECTOR	CREATIVE DIRECTOR	ROYAL HOUSEHOLD
Tom Corby MVO	*Stewart Lee*	*David Hicks*	*Victoria Tuke*
SUB EDITOR	ADVERTISING PRODUCTION	PUBLISHING EDITOR, RCT	HEAD OF PUBLISHING, RCT
Justyn Barnes	*Angela Brown*	*Polly Fellows*	*Kate Owen*

Whilst every care has been taken in compiling this publication, and the statements contained herein are believed to be correct, the publishers and the promoters will not accept responsibility for any inaccuracies. Reproduction of any part of this publication without permission is strictly forbidden. ©Publications UK LTD 2022. The Royal Household, Royal Collection Trust and the publishers make no recommendation in respect of any of the advertisers, and no recommendation may be implied by way of the presence of their advertisements. Printed by Micropress Printers Ltd. Distributed by Seymour Distribution Ltd.

PICTURE CREDITS
The publisher and its partners are grateful for permission to reproduce the items listed below:

Cover: Royal Collection Trust/ © Her Majesty Queen Elizabeth II 2022
Page 2: © Chris Jackson/Getty Images
Page 4: © Hugo Burnand
Page 11: © Yousuf Karsh/Camera Press
Pages 12, 13, 14, 18, 19, 20, 21, 22, 23, 24, 25, 26, 27, 44, 46, 48, 50, 51, 52, 53, 55, 56, 58, 59, 60, 61, 62, 63, 64, 65, 66, 67, 71, 80, 82 © PA/Alamy
Pages 28, 29: © Fortnum & Mason
Pages 34–41: unless otherwise stated, text and all works reproduced are Royal Collection Trust/© Her Majesty Queen Elizabeth II 2022
Page 35: Royal Collection Trust/ © Her Majesty Queen Elizabeth II 2022. Photographer: Peter Smith
Pages 39, 41, 42, 63 (main image), 70 (all): Royal Collection Trust/All Rights Reserved
Page 43: © Baron/Camera Press
Page 49: © Cecil Beaton/Camera Press
Page 57: © Matt Holyoak/Camera Press
Pages 69, 72, 73: Royal Collection Trust/© Her Majesty Queen Elizabeth II 2022
Page 76: Adobe Stock/PA
Page 78: © 2021 Picture Plane/Heatherwick Studio, all rights reserved

Congratulations to Her Majesty

THE QUEEN

Leading our nation for years

WAITROSE
& PARTNERS

– PROUD TO CELEBRATE –
THE QUEEN'S PLATINUM JUBILEE

BOODLES
1798

A FAMILY STORY

Yasmin and Amber Le Bon wear Raindance

PROUD PARTNER OF

Her Majesty The Queen's
PLATINUM JUBILEE PAGEANT
1952 – 2022

INTRODUCTION

HER MAJESTY THE QUEEN'S PLATINUM JUBILEE

Thursday 2 June – Sunday 5 June

On 6 February 2022 Her Majesty The Queen became the first British monarch to celebrate a Platinum Jubilee, marking 70 years of service to the people of the United Kingdom, her other Realms and the Commonwealth. To celebrate this unprecedented anniversary, events and initiatives will take place throughout the year, culminating in a four-day Bank Holiday weekend.

How typical of The Queen to sign her Platinum Jubilee address to the nation with the simple, but telling, words: "Your Servant. Elizabeth R." It sums up a core theme of her long reign: an exemplary, deep-rooted sense of duty.

In 1947, as Princess Elizabeth, she pledged that her whole life would be devoted to "your service". The Princess was speaking from her heart; she meant it then, and she means it now. The Queen has never wavered throughout the seven decades of her reign, gently adapting the institution she so nobly heads to the tide of social change. Her Majesty is confident and optimistic about the future and the opportunities it will offer. At the same time, she wants to express heartfelt thanks for the support she has received in her task, and remains, in her own words, "eternally grateful for, and humbled by the loyalty and affection that you continue to give me".

The Queen is the figurehead of the ship of state, but, above politics, is often referred to as one of the most respected figures in public life, acclaimed across the world; a reassuring and enduring source of stability, security and inspiration. Her people have much cause to be grateful, particularly in this her Platinum Jubilee year, when we mark the seven decades of her reign with celebrations all over this country and in the Commonwealth.

She became our Queen unexpectedly because of the dynastic crisis caused by the abdication of her uncle, King Edward VIII, and the premature death of her father, King George VI. Only 25 years old at the time, the Princess rose admirably to the occasion: even at that very young age, she was deeply conscious of the magic of monarchy, its significance as a focus of national loyalties and in its spheres of influence. The Platinum Jubilee celebrations will, in their different ways, reflect this, providing an opportunity to express the very personal relationship between Crown and country. ✦ **Tom Corby MVO**

THE QUEEN'S BIRTHDAY PARADE – TROOPING THE COLOUR

SOLDIERS OF THE QUEEN

The Queen's Birthday Parade – Trooping the Colour, Thursday 2 June

Trooping the Colour – when more than 850 soldiers, 200 horses and 300 musicians will come together in the traditional Parade to mark The Queen's Official Birthday.

The Queen's Birthday Parade is an occasion of precision, pageantry, fanfares and drumbeats, and on 2 June it signals the start of the Platinum Jubilee celebrations. The colour that is being trooped this year is that of the 1st Battalion Irish Guards. More than 1,150 officers and soldiers of the Royal Household Division are taking part. Also on parade, leading the Irish Guards band, will be the regimental mascot Turlough Mór, an Irish Wolfhound named after an ancient Irish king.

On this very special day, the troops are paying a personal tribute to their Sovereign and Colonel-in-Chief. It is a personal moment for Her Majesty too. The then Princess Elizabeth made her debut, mounted, as Royal Colonel of the Grenadier Guards in 1947. In 1951, when her father, King George VI, was unable to take the salute himself due to illness, she took his place, and thereafter has been at the saluting base for virtually every year of her reign. There is no one who is more expert on every detail of the Trooping the Colour ceremony than The Queen. Her Majesty expects perfection and gets it.

For 18 consecutive years, The Queen rode Burmese, a gift to her from the Royal Canadian Mounted Police. Burmese retired to Windsor, and thereafter The Queen decided that rather than train another horse for this distinguished role, she would be driven in a carriage that had been built for Queen Victoria in 1842. Flanking Her Majesty's carriage will be three Royal Colonels: The Prince of Wales, the Welsh Guards; The Duke of Cambridge, the Irish Guards; and The Princess Royal, the Blues and Royals. ✦

1981 The Queen on her long-serving horse, Burmese, during the Trooping the Colour ceremony in London.

Soldiers will make their way from Buckingham Palace to Horse Guards Parade, in London, ahead of the Trooping the Colour ceremony, as Her Majesty Queen Elizabeth II celebrates her Official Birthday.

PLATINUM JUBILEE BEACONS

THE QUEEN'S PLATINUM JUBILEE BEACONS
2ND JUNE 2022

THE UNITED KINGDOM & THE COMMONWEALTH, ILLUMINATED

Thursday 2 June

The United Kingdom and the Commonwealth will be illuminated by a blaze of light when the Platinum Jubilee Beacons are ignited on the evening of 2 June. More than 1,500 towns, villages and cities throughout Britain, the Channel Islands, the Isle of Man and the UK's overseas territories will join in lighting beacons. Beacons will also be started in each of the capital cities of Commonwealth countries. The principal beacon will be lit in a special ceremony at Buckingham Palace. Bruno Peek, the Beacon Pageant Master, promises a night to remember.

The tradition of beacon lighting to celebrate royal weddings, jubilees and coronations dates back hundreds of years. Beacon chains were also once used for sending messages at times of national peril, such as the threat of the Spanish Armada. They formed the backdrop to the rallying speech of the first Queen Elizabeth, when she told her troops in 1588: "I know I have the body of a weak and feeble woman, but I have the heart and stomach of a king, and of a king of England too, and think foul scorn that Parma or Spain, or any prince of Europe, should dare to invade the borders of my realm." It worked, but the beacons also played their part.

Beacons have since become symbols of unity across borders, countries and continents. In 1897, beacons were lit nationally to celebrate Queen Victoria's Diamond Jubilee. In 1977, 2002 and 2012 they illuminated the country to celebrate our Queen's Silver, Golden and Diamond Jubilees. ✦

For more information please visit
queensjubileebeacons.com

The official beacon lit by Her Majesty The Queen at Windsor Castle to celebrate her 90th birthday in 2016.

There are three types of official beacons being lit for Her Majesty's Platinum Jubilee: a freestanding gas-fuelled beacon *(opposite)*, a beacon brazier with a metal shield *(this page)* and a bonfire beacon. Communities with pre-existing beacons are encouraged to light these on the evening of 2 June.

SERVICE OF THANKSGIVING

St Paul's Cathedral, Friday 3 June

The Queen and other members of the Royal Family will attend the Platinum Jubilee Service of Thanksgiving at St Paul's Cathedral on 3 June. This will be the fourth Jubilee thanksgiving in Her Majesty's seven-decade reign. The first marked the Silver Jubilee in 1977, followed by the Golden Jubilee in 2002 and Diamond in 2012.

10 June 2016 The Service of Thanksgiving held to mark the 90th birthday of The Queen at St Paul's Cathedral, London.

St Paul's is the venue for many national events and has been the natural setting for royal celebrations throughout history. One of the first was in 1789, when a service of thanksgiving was held to mark the return to health of George III. This was followed by the thanksgiving service in 1897 for the 60-year reign of Queen Victoria. The short service was held in front of the cathedral for the Queen's comfort as she was unable to walk up the steps. King George V's Silver Jubilee in 1935 was another royal landmark for St Paul's.

The Platinum Jubilee service will include bible readings, anthems, prayers and hymns through which the invited congregation of over 2,000 will express their thankfulness for The Queen's reign. The congregation will include those who have been identified as having given outstanding contributions to their local communities from across the United Kingdom. Children chosen from the length and breadth of the land, and from the countries of which The Queen is Head of State, will lead an Act of Hope and Commitment. The programme will also feature a new anthem composed by Judith Weir, the Master of The Queen's Music, which sets words from the third chapter of the Book of Proverbs to music.

The service will be led by the Dean of St Paul's, the Bishop of London and the Archbishop of Canterbury, who will give the address. Church leaders from across the country, together with leaders of other faiths and denominations, will attend. The service will be broadcast live on television and radio. ✦

3 June 2002 The Queen waves to the crowd as she rides with The Duke of Edinburgh in the Gold State Coach from Buckingham Palace to St Paul's Cathedral for a Service of Thanksgiving to celebrate her Golden Jubilee.

THE EPSOM DERBY

Below: **2 June 1965**
The Queen walking back from the paddock after viewing the runners for the 1965 Derby.

THE EPSOM DERBY

Friday 3 June – Saturday 4 June

The Queen's lifelong relationship with the world's greatest flat race, the Epsom Derby, began in 1946, when a few weeks after her 20th birthday the then Princess Elizabeth accompanied her father, King George VI, to the Epsom course. Thereafter she became one of its greatest fans and supporters. Princess Elizabeth had a deep interest in anything equine, and the Royal Family had long been closely involved in British horse racing, often having runners in the top races.

After her Coronation in 1953, one of The Queen's first actions was to award a knighthood to the renowned jockey Gordon Richards. The death of her father in 1952 meant that she inherited one of the finest collections of breeding and racing stock in the world, and jockeys wearing her purple and scarlet colours have won more than 1,600 races. Horses owned by The Queen have won most of the British classics, some multiple times, but victory in the Derby as an owner has eluded Her Majesty.

The Queen invariably derives huge enjoyment from the Derby, and at the time of her Diamond Jubilee the Coronation Cup was renamed the Diamond Jubilee Coronation Cup. It was a fitting tribute to her love of the turf. In 1900, the winning horse in the Derby was called Diamond Jubilee. It had been bought by the Prince of Wales, later King Edward VII, as a tribute to his mother, Queen Victoria, for her landmark 60-year Jubilee celebration in 1897. Attending the races is one of our Queen's favourite pastimes, and she is often seen cheering on her favourite, like any other race goer.

This year Her Majesty has entered three of her horses in the Derby as she attempts to win the most prestigious horse race for the first time. Among her trio of hopefuls is 'Reaching for the Moon', one of her equine stars in 2021 when he won the Group 3 Solario Stakes at Sandown Park and finished second in the Group 2 Champagne Stakes at Doncaster. He has been touted as a possible Derby horse and is not only owned by The Queen, but was also bred at the Royal Stud at Sandringham, her Norfolk estate. Another potential Derby runner is 'Educator', also both owned and bred by Her Majesty. The third of The Queen's Derby hopefuls is 'General Idea', sired by the late 'Galileo', the most sought-after sire in the world.

This year the Epsom Derby is poised to celebrate The Queen's Platinum Jubilee, making the event even more special. No race on earth is quite like the Derby. It has a touch of carnival, and is for everyone – from racing royalty to racing rookies. ✦

7 June 2014
The Queen casts her expert eye over Australia, ridden by Joseph O'Brien, in the parade ring before the Epsom Derby.

PLATINUM JUBILEE CONCERT

PLATINUM PARTY AT THE PALACE

Saturday 4 June

The Platinum Party at the Palace promises to be an occasion to remember, playing a central part in a weekend of pageantry, parades and street parties. It will be broadcast live on BBC 1, BBC iPlayer and across the entire BBC network.

PLATINUM JUBILEE CONCERT

A star-studded line-up of artists, bands and entertainers from across music, film and theatre are ready to give you the show of a lifetime, celebrating Her Majesty's Platinum Jubilee at Buckingham Palace. The award-winning singer George Ezra has confirmed that he'll be performing on the night, with more fantastic artists to be announced shortly. "I can't begin to tell you how excited I am to be part of The Queen's Platinum Jubilee concert, what an incredible honour to be asked," the 28-year-old singer said in a statement, adding he plans to "bring pop and roll to the Palace".

Jubilee concerts on such an impressive scale are an innovative form of tribute. The Queen's Golden Jubilee Concert in 2002 featured a programme of iconic music legends, with Queen guitarist, Brian May, perched on the roof of Buckingham Palace, electrifying the audience with his arrangement of *God Save The Queen*.

Ten years later, the Diamond Jubilee Concert was a spectacular celebration of 60 years of The Queen's reign through music, including the best of rock and pop performed by world-famous British artists including Sir Paul McCartney, Sir Elton John, Dame Shirley Bassey, Sir Tom Jones and Sir Cliff Richard. The show featured memorable and extraordinary collaborations between the performers, many of them from across the Commonwealth, alongside gems from musical theatre and classical music. In a speech at the end of the concert, The Prince of Wales gave a moving tribute to The Queen, calling for three "resounding cheers for a very special person". The audience responded with delight.

In this Platinum Jubilee year, many special events are being staged nationwide. The first of many such high-profile events was "The Queen's Platinum Jubilee 70 Years Concert", which took place at the Royal Albert Hall on 16 March. The event was promoted by SSAFA, the Armed Forces charity.

Chart-topping singer George Ezra, with his breezy style and constant smile, will be one of the artists performing on the night.

The concert also marked the 70th anniversary of The Queen's patronage of the organisation.

The programme focused on the music played at Her Majesty's Coronation in 1953, featuring a repertoire by British composers including Edward Elgar, Vaughan Williams, Benjamin Britten and William Walton, performed by the Royal Philharmonic Concert Orchestra.

Final numbers are to be confirmed, but so far more than 700 celebratory public events and almost 1,000 street parties will be held across the United Kingdom to mark the Platinum Jubilee. ♦

For more information visit **platinumjubilee.gov.uk/event/platinum-party-at-the-palace/**

Queen guitarist Brian May, performing *God Save The Queen* on the roof of Buckingham Palace, as part of the Golden Jubilee Concert in 2002.

Dame Shirley Bassey performing one of her many hits in 2012.

Singer-songwriter Ed Sheeran on the main stage back in 2012.

4 June 2012 The Queen is greeted by The Prince of Wales, as they are joined on stage with the rest of the Royal family and a host of global pop stars and performers at the end of the Diamond Jubilee Concert at Buckingham Palace.

THE BIG JUBILEE LUNCH

Thursday 2 June – Sunday 5 June

The Big Jubilee Lunch, of which The Duchess of Cornwall is Patron, aims to inspire community spirit throughout the United Kingdom. The initiative offers the opportunity to share friendship, food and fun with neighbours. It can take the form of a small get-together in the back garden, a park or driveway, or a larger party with trestle tables down the middle of the street.

Thousands of people and organisations have signed up to host a lunch and there will be flagship lunches in London, with the Eden Project, the social enterprise charity in Cornwall, co-ordinating the project.

There is a rich tradition of holding street parties to celebrate royal landmarks such as The Queen's Coronation in 1953, her previous jubilees in 1977 and 2002 and notably her Diamond Jubilee in 2012. Dipping into history, the end of the Second World War was marked by spontaneous street parties up and down the country.

The Big Jubilee Lunch's organisers claim, quite rightly, that every event will be unique, creating a memory that will last a lifetime; a cultural bond that inspires neighbours to become lasting friends, even if their particular lunch is just a sandwich or a cup of tea on the doorstep. So come and join the fun! ✦

THE PLATINUM PUDDING COMPETITION

A JUBILEE PUDDING FIT FOR A QUEEN

Winners to be announced on 12 May

We've had Victoria sponge, named after Queen Victoria, and said to be her favourite piece of cake. Then there was Coronation Chicken (or 'poulet Reine Elizabeth'), created by Constance Spry and Rosemary Hume, to be served at the Coronation banquet in 1953.

In 2021, The Platinum Pudding Competition was launched by Fortnum & Mason to find a pudding to celebrate The Queen's 70-year reign. Thousands of recipes have now been judged by an independent panel of expert judges comprising award-winning home bakers, professional chefs, authors, historians and patissiers, including author and television presenter Dame Mary Berry; Mark Flanagan LVO, the Royal Chef; and Roger Pizey, Fortnum & Mason's Executive Pastry Chef. The winning recipe is available to follow at *fortnumandmason.com/platinum-pudding* and will be served at Big Jubilee Lunches up and down the country. ✦

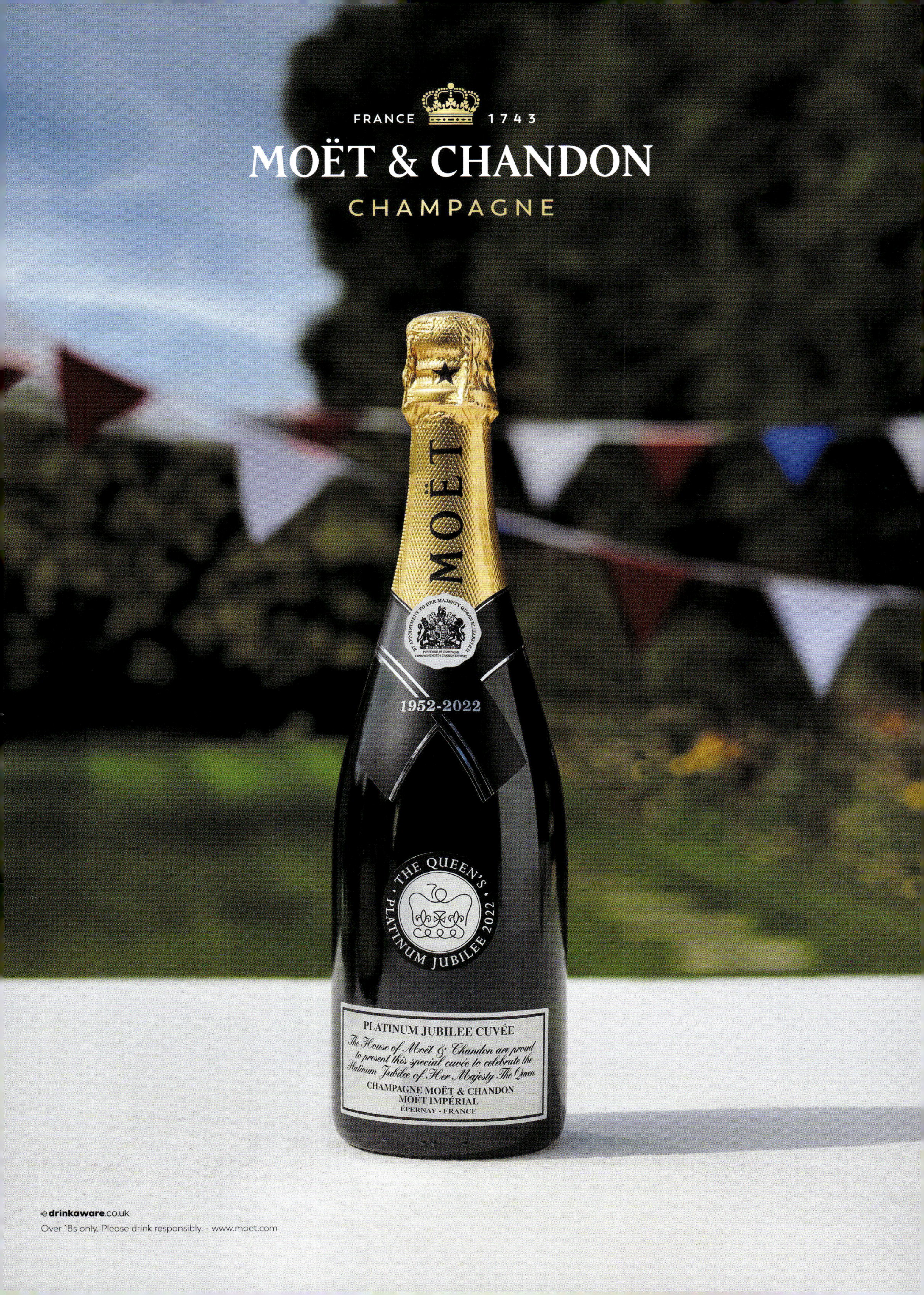
FRANCE 1743
MOËT & CHANDON
CHAMPAGNE
MOËT
1952-2022
THE QUEEN'S PLATINUM JUBILEE 2022
PLATINUM JUBILEE CUVÉE
The House of Moët & Chandon are proud to present this special cuvée to celebrate the Platinum Jubilee of Her Majesty The Queen.
CHAMPAGNE MOËT & CHANDON
MOËT IMPÉRIAL
ÉPERNAY - FRANCE
drinkaware.co.uk
Over 18s only. Please drink responsibly. - www.moet.com

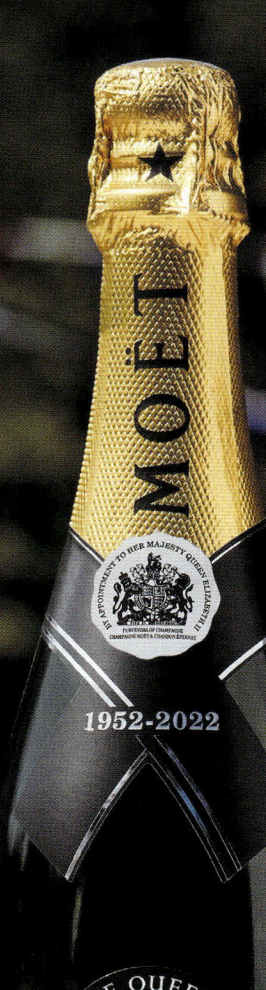

THE PLATINUM PUDDING COMPETITION

Above: **1 March 2012** The Queen, The Duchess of Cornwall and The Duchess of Cambridge visited Fortnum & Mason and were given a tour of its famous food hall. A plaque to commemorate the regeneration of the local Piccadilly area was unveiled by The Queen.

Above: **1 March 2012** The Queen, The Duchess of Cornwall and The Duchess of Cambridge enjoying a closer look inside a selection of Fortnum & Mason's famous handwoven wicker hampers.

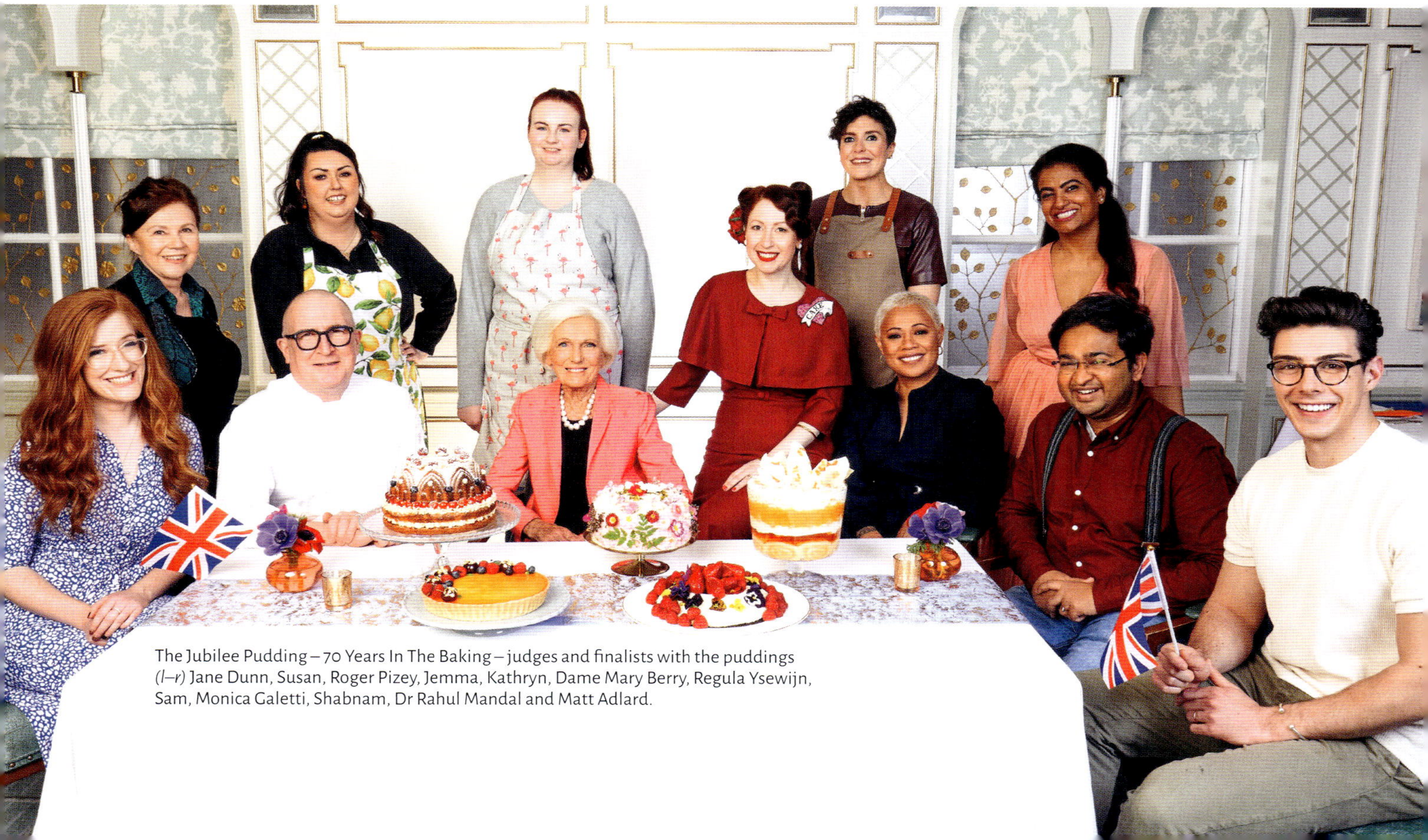

The Jubilee Pudding – 70 Years In The Baking – judges and finalists with the puddings (l–r) Jane Dunn, Susan, Roger Pizey, Jemma, Kathryn, Dame Mary Berry, Regula Ysewijn, Sam, Monica Galetti, Shabnam, Dr Rahul Mandal and Matt Adlard.

A TOAST TO 70 GLORIOUS YEARS

Whispering Angel

A Proud Partner of

Her Majesty The Queen's
PLATINUM JUBILEE PAGEANT
1952 – 2022

Wine, © 2022 Moët Hennessy UK, Inc., London, Please Drink Responsibly

THE PLATINUM JUBILEE PAGEANT

Her Majesty The Queen's
PLATINUM JUBILEE PAGEANT
1952 – 2022

THE PLATINUM JUBILEE PAGEANT 1952–2022

Sunday 5 June, London

The Platinum Jubilee Pageant will tell the story of The Queen's reign and how the United Kingdom has changed over the past 70 years in one of the largest celebratory events in recent years. It will combine pomp and ceremony, street art and cutting-edge visual technology, drawing on talent from every part of the United Kingdom and the Commonwealth.

Act I: For Queen and Country is the opening act of the Platinum Jubilee Pageant. It will be a military spectacle, celebrating the UK Armed Forces from all three Services, along with military personnel from across the Commonwealth including Canada, New Zealand, Australia, Pakistan, Ghana, Belize, Jamaica, Sri Lanka, and beyond.

Act II: The Time of Our Lives is a vibrant display of British life since 1952, moving through a transformation of popular culture over the last 70 years.

Act III: Let's Celebrate. The third act of the Platinum Jubilee Pageant, Let's Celebrate, will harness creativity, ingenuity, humour and community spirit.

Act IV: Happy and Glorious. A finale like no other will form around the Queen Victoria Memorial in front of Buckingham Palace with all parts of the Pageant leading to this moment. It will serve as an opportunity to gather and pay tribute to Her Majesty with the singing of the National Anthem, 'God Save the Queen' and a gospel choir to the sounds of the Band of Her Majesty's Royal Marines.

Members of the viewing public will be invited to become part of the finale, as they gather outside the gates of Buckingham Palace to watch national treasures from the world of the performing arts, entertainment, fashion, business and media, including Jeremy Irons, Bill Bailey and Gok Wan. The entertainment will be led by one of the world's bestselling music artists, Ed Sheeran.

The finale will also include the River of Hope, performed by schoolchildren processing down The Mall with two hundred silk flags *(left)*, appearing like a moving river. Schoolchildren have been invited to create imaginative artworks using only natural or recycled materials, and focused on climate change and protecting their own natural environment. All the artworks submitted from around the world will be displayed online as part of the celebrations. ✦

THE PLATINUM JUBILEE AT THE ROYAL RESIDENCES

Sunday 3 July – Sunday 2 October

Three special displays marking significant occasions in Her Majesty's reign – the Accession, the Coronation and her Jubilees – will be staged at the official royal residences in 2022.

The Royal Collection is one of the largest and most prestigious art collections in the world. It is a treasure trove of works of art accumulated over the centuries by a succession of monarchs, reflecting royal tastes from the Tudors to the present day. The Royal Collection is not owned personally by The Queen but is held in trust by her as Sovereign for her successors and the nation. It is conserved and cared for by the specialists who work for Royal Collection Trust.

Many great artists from the past are represented, including Leonardo, Holbein, Vermeer, Rubens, Rembrandt, Artemisia Gentileschi and Canaletto. And the decorative arts: furniture, ceramics, silver and gold plate, sculpture and tapestries, are all splendidly represented.

The furniture – much of it dating from the 17th to the 19th centuries – is outstanding, most notably the French furniture of the 18th century that found its way into the Collection after the upheaval of the French Revolution when the palaces and châteaux of the aristocracy were emptied. The armour would equip a regiment of princes, and there are many mementos of our country's past, including the bullet that killed Lord Nelson at the Battle of Trafalgar.

Since the 16th century rulers have left their mark on the Collection, especially Charles I and George IV, both keen connoisseurs with an eye for art. As the leading collector of his age, George spent heavily and extravagantly, but to excellent effect. Charles I was one of the greatest royal patrons of all time, who lovingly collected and cherished his great works of art. Charles I's discovery of Titian on his visit to Spain in 1623 when Prince of Wales encouraged a lifelong passion for Italian art. The king's patronage of artists, including Rubens and Van Dyck, revolutionised painting in England, creating royal portraits that endure today as powerful images of Charles I, his family and his kingship.

During The Queen's reign the Collection has continued to grow with the acquisition of historical and modern works of art. One of Her Majesty's most significant contributions to the arts has been the creation of The Queen's Gallery, built on the ruins of the former private chapel on the west front of Buckingham Palace, destroyed by a German bombing raid in 1940. Originally opened in the 1960s, the Gallery was enlarged in 2002 as part of the celebrations for The Queen's Golden Jubilee and along with its companion Gallery at the Palace of Holyroodhouse, also built in 2002, hosts a regular programme of special exhibitions showcasing items from the Royal Collection.

The Collection is spread among some 15 royal residences and former residences across the UK, most of which are regularly open to the public. A visit to the exhibitions mounted by the Trust would fire anyone's imagination. ✦

The Queen's Drawing Room, one of the many rooms containing items from the Royal Collection that are open to visitors at Windsor Castle.

One of the iconic portraits of The Queen, photographed by Dorothy Wilding, that will go on display at Buckingham Palace this summer. Her Majesty is wearing the Girls of Great Britain and Ireland Tiara.

The first official photographic sitting with the new queen was commissioned by the Post Office and Royal Mint. It took place on 26 February 1952, just 20 days after the Accession.

THE PLATINUM JUBILEE AT THE ROYAL RESIDENCES

PLATINUM JUBILEE: THE QUEEN'S ACCESSION

Buckingham Palace, 22 July – 2 October

At the Summer Opening of the State Rooms at Buckingham Palace, the display on The Queen's Accession will include portraits of The Queen taken by Dorothy Wilding, alongside items of Her Majesty's personal jewellery worn for the portrait sittings.

Queen Elizabeth II is not the only monarch of England to have reached a historic milestone in their reign: as early as the 13th century a 50-year reign was achieved by Henry III (r. 1216–72), followed in the 14th century by Edward III (r. 1327–77) and later, in the 16th century by James VI of Scotland and I of England (r. 1566–1625). The Queen's namesake, Elizabeth I, reigned for 45 years, from 1558 to 1603. We have few, if any, records relating to how these milestones were marked in royal or national life until the reign of George III, whose Golden Jubilee in 1809 was marked by a service of thanksgiving. In the 19th century Queen Victoria enjoyed a remarkably long reign, the second longest in British history, celebrating the very first Diamond Jubilee in 1897, which was marked by many celebratory events and commemorative souvenirs. In this most historic of years, marking Queen Elizabeth II's Platinum Jubilee, the first in British history, the events will be marked at Buckingham Palace, Windsor Castle and the Palace of Holyroodhouse by a series of special exhibitions, each display reflecting a different aspect of The Queen's reign.

At Buckingham Palace, for the annual Summer Opening of the State Rooms, the display will focus on the very beginning of Her Majesty's reign, featuring the Accession portrait photographs taken by Dorothy Wilding in 1952. Just 20 days after the death of King George VI, a sitting was granted to Wilding to produce the first ever official portraits of the new queen. These were required for use on coinage and postage stamps, for the dissemination of official imagery around the United Kingdom and the Commonwealth, and for display in every British embassy overseas. Wilding had become the first official female royal photographer when she was appointed to take portraits at the coronation of King George VI and Queen Elizabeth, in 1937, and she enjoyed a prolific career spanning more than 40 years as the leading female British portrait photographer of her day.

Dressed in a black velvet evening gown, designed by the couturier Norman Hartnell, The Queen was photographed at Clarence House in a series of poses wearing different jewels, including a diamond necklace presented by the Government of the Union of South Africa for her 21st birthday, and the Girls of Great Britain and Ireland Tiara, given first to Queen Mary, when Duchess of York, as a wedding present in 1893, and then presented as a gift to her granddaughter, Princess Elizabeth, for her wedding to Prince Philip in 1947.

A few weeks later, in April 1952, a second set of portraits marking The Queen's Accession was taken by Wilding, this time with The Queen dressed in a silk velvet and damask gown and, significantly, wearing the Diamond Diadem, a regal circlet originally made by the royal jewellers, Rundell, Bridge & Rundell, and supplied for the coronation of George IV in 1820. This diadem, a highly important diamond and pearl jewel, was considered appropriate for reproduction of The Queen's image on postage stamps and coinage, given that her Coronation had not yet taken place and it was not therefore possible for a crown to be worn.

The original prints created and supplied by Wilding will be displayed together for the first time at Buckingham Palace, alongside the jewels from Her Majesty's personal collection that can be seen in the portraits. The photographs show Wilding's mastery of lighting and retouching, together with her ability to create powerful and emblematic portraits that would become the most important and iconic images of at least the first quarter century of The Queen's reign. ✦

THE PLATINUM JUBILEE AT THE ROYAL RESIDENCES

PLATINUM JUBILEE: THE QUEEN'S CORONATION

Windsor Castle, 7 July – 26 September

At Windsor Castle, the Coronation Dress and Robe of Estate worn by The Queen for her Coronation at Westminster Abbey on 2 June 1953 will be on display.

At Windsor Castle, Royal Collection Trust's exhibition will commemorate another highly significant occasion in The Queen's reign, Her Majesty's Coronation, which took place at Westminster Abbey on 2 June 1953. The centrepieces of the display will be the Coronation Dress and the Robe of Estate, each specially designed and created for the occasion and combining both tradition and modernity, together with the personal wishes of the Sovereign in their design and execution.

The Coronation Dress is regarded as one of the most important examples of 20th-century British couture and was entrusted to Norman Hartnell, who was principal designer by appointment to Queen Elizabeth The Queen Mother and to Her Majesty The Queen. Hartnell had begun to supply clothes for Princess Elizabeth from the early 1940s and his most notable commission was for her wedding dress in 1947. He submitted a total of nine designs to The Queen, based on extensive historical research and taking into account the setting in which this unique dress would be worn, including live television footage. The 1953 Coronation was the first to be fully televised: it was broadcast live by the BBC and watched by millions in the United Kingdom and around the world.

The iconography of embroidered emblems on the silk satin of the dress includes not only those of the four nations of the United Kingdom but also of the six other independent states of which The Queen was monarch and head of state at the time of her Accession.

The magnificent Robe of Estate, worn for the procession out of Westminster Abbey following the Coronation ceremony, was made by the firm of Ede & Ravenscroft, of Chancery Lane, London, makers of coronation robes to the monarchy since the coronation of George III in 1761. It is made of fine purple silk velvet and was embroidered by the Royal School of Needlework in goldwork embroidery, featuring 18 different types of gold thread. It took 12 embroideresses more than 3,500 hours to complete the design of a border of entwined wheat ears and olive branches, symbolising prosperity and peace, together with The Queen's crowned 'ER' cypher. The Coronation Dress and Robe of Estate will be displayed alongside the state portrait of Her Majesty in her coronation robes, which was completed by the artist Sir Herbert James Gunn in 1954. Gunn's painting conforms to the tradition of state portraits, particularly following those of Queen Alexandra and Queen Mary, and depicts The Queen standing on a dais wearing the Coronation Dress, Robe of Estate and Diamond Diadem, adjacent to a table bearing the Imperial State Crown and the Sovereign's Sceptre. Every detail is exquisitely executed in Gunn's meticulous style, including the light falling on the diamond 'Coronation' necklace, originally made for Queen Victoria in 1858, and The Queen's own insignia of the Order of the Garter, both of which will be displayed at Windsor Castle.

The national emblems painstakingly embroidered onto the Coronation dress will also be present in a different form in the display at Windsor. During The Queen's historic Coronation Tour of the Commonwealth from November 1953 to May 1954, which covered more than 40,000 miles, a number of important jewels representing national emblems in the form of brooches were given as gifts to The Queen. These historic brooches have been regularly worn by Her Majesty during her 70-year reign, on national days and on visits to the countries by which they were presented, and will be brought together as part of the display for the first time. ✦

The Coronation Dress and the Robe of Estate worn by The Queen for her Coronation on 2 June 1953. The gown has short sleeves, a sweetheart neckline and a full circular skirt embroidered with crystals, pearls, sequins and silk thread depicting the national emblems of Great Britain and countries of the Commonwealth.

THE PLATINUM JUBILEE AT THE ROYAL RESIDENCES

ROYAL COLLECTION TRUST

PLATINUM JUBILEE DISPLAY

Palace of Holyroodhouse, 3 July – 25 September

At the Palace of Holyroodhouse, visitors will see a display of outfits worn by Her Majesty on occasions to celebrate the Silver, Golden and Diamond Jubilees.

The Queen's historic achievement of marking four Jubilees during her reign – Silver, Golden, Diamond and Platinum – will be commemorated in the display at the Palace of Holyroodhouse in Edinburgh, The Queen's official residence in Scotland. Ensembles worn by Her Majesty for the services of thanksgiving, held at St Paul's Cathedral in London, will be shown together for the first time. Alongside the outfits, the display will include items associated with The Queen's first visit as Sovereign to Scotland in June 1953, together with gifts from Scottish institutions and official engagements carried out in Scotland over the seven decades of Her Majesty's reign. Reflecting a breadth of historic and social change in the country since the Accession in 1952, these will include a miner's lamp from The Queen's first descent into a working coal mine in Fife in 1958, a glass curling stone from the opening of the Aberdeen Curling Rink in 1983 and a model of the Queensferry Crossing, across the Firth of Forth, opened by The Queen in 2017. In addition to the display within the Palace, a further exhibition staged in The Queen's Gallery, Edinburgh, during the Platinum Jubilee year, comprises masterpieces from Buckingham Palace. Presented together for the first time in Scotland in a modern gallery setting, the exhibition showcases some of the greatest paintings in the Royal Collection, including portraits, landscapes and genre scenes by such renowned masters as Rembrandt, Van Dyck, Rubens and Artemisia Gentileschi. ◆

The special exhibition *Masterpieces from Buckingham Palace* includes notable Italian paintings such as *Pallas Athene* (c.1531–8) by Parmigianino *(left)* and atmospheric landscapes including *Harbour Scene at Sunset* (1643) by Claude Lorrain *(below)*.

The display of masterpieces from the Royal Collection features Rembrandt van Rijn's striking 1641 portrait of Agatha Bas.

The Queen's Silver Jubilee dress, coat and hat will be on display at the Palace of Holyroodhouse as part of the Royal Collection's celebration of the Platinum Jubilee. For the Service of Thanksgiving held at St Paul's Cathedral on 7 June 1977, The Queen wore this pink ensemble, designed by one of her favourite dressmakers, Hardy Amies, and complemented by a playfully designed hat created by her long-time milliner, Frederick Fox, which features 25 stylised flowerheads hanging from silk threads.

HER MAJESTY QUEEN ELIZABETH II

The story of her seven decades – the country's longest-reigning monarch.

A ROYAL WEDDING

Princess Elizabeth and Prince Philip of Greece and Denmark were married on 20 November 1947. The scene in Westminster Abbey was dazzling, a splash of colour in a bleak, monochrome post-war world. As well as food and clothes rationing, a bitterly cold winter had caused a fuel crisis and the nation shivered. The country welcomed the royal wedding as a much-needed distraction from the numbing restrictions that hedged in their lives.

It was agreed that the wedding should not be ostentatious – Princess Elizabeth even used clothing ration coupons to pay for her dress – but nevertheless London took on a carnival atmosphere and crowds lined the streets to wish the couple well. They received 10,000 telegrams of congratulations, and more than 2,500 wedding presents poured in from around the world, 1,500 of which went on public display at St James's Palace. Two thousand guests, including foreign royalty, were invited to attend the ceremony, which was broadcast by BBC Radio to around 200 million listeners worldwide.

9 July 1947 Smiling happily, the Princess and her fiancé, Lieutenant Philip Mountbatten, were pictured at Buckingham Palace on the day their engagement was officially announced.

20 November 1947 The newly married royal couple on their wedding day at Buckingham Palace.

Like Princess Elizabeth, the bridegroom was a great-great-grandchild of Queen Victoria. Born on the Greek island of Corfu to Prince Andrew of Greece and Princess Alice of Battenberg, Prince Philip had connections to several royal families of Europe through both parents. Due to the unstable political situation in Greece in the early 1920s, the family spent much of Prince Philip's young life in exile in Paris.

He served in the Royal Navy during the war, becoming a naturalised British citizen on 18 March 1947. He relinquished his Greek and Danish royal titles and, taking the family name of his maternal grandfather, became Lieutenant Philip Mountbatten, RN. On the eve of his marriage he was named His Royal Highness The Duke of Edinburgh and created Baron Greenwich, Earl of Merioneth. The King had earlier appointed him a Knight of the Garter, Britain's oldest order of chivalry.

The bride's wedding gown was of ivory duchesse satin. More than 10,000 seed pearls, imported from the United States of America, had gone into its making. The couple's honeymoon was split between two locations: Broadlands, in Hampshire, the home of Philip's uncle, Lord Mountbatten, and Birkhall, on the Balmoral estate.

They returned home three weeks later, in time for the King's 52nd birthday on 14 December. "The Edinburghs are back from Scotland," noted the Princess's Private Secretary, John Colville, adding that the Princess "was looking very happy".

20 November 1947 The royal couple appear on the Buckingham Palace balcony, to wave at the thousands gathered below in The Mall.

23 November 1947 The Duke and Duchess of Edinburgh, as the couple were now known, pictured during their honeymoon at Broadlands, Hampshire.

CONGRATULATIONS MA'AM
ON YOUR
PLATINUM JUBILEE
FROM
M&S

We salute you!

THE QUEEN'S REIGN

ACCESSION

King George VI was only 56 when he died in February 1952. The last years of his life had been an anxious time for the then Princess Elizabeth and Prince Philip as the full gravity of the King's prolonged illness, with its implications, was brought home to them. After their marriage the young couple divided their time between Britain and Malta, where Prince Philip was stationed on naval duties. But in July 1951 they left Malta for good, as the King's health was increasingly poor and Princess Elizabeth was required to take on more of his public duties.

In early 1952, recovery from recent surgery prevented the King from undertaking a long-planned major tour of the Commonwealth. The trip to East Africa, Australia and New Zealand was left in the capable hands of Princess Elizabeth and Prince Philip. The King waved them off at London Airport on 31 January. It was a bitterly raw day, but he stood windswept on the tarmac, straining his eyes to watch the steady climb of the Argonaut aircraft. It was the last farewell.

The following day he returned with Queen Elizabeth and Princess Margaret to Sandringham, the royal family's Norfolk estate. Sadly the King passed away in his sleep on the night of 5/6 February.

Three thousand miles away in Kenya, Princess Elizabeth was informed of her father's death at Sagana Lodge, to which the royal couple had just returned, having spent the previous night in a treetop cabin at the Treetops Hotel, set in a giant fig tree, watching rhinoceroses, elephants and waterbucks drinking from a water hole in the Aberdare Forest game reserve. As one observer wrote: "A young girl climbed into a tree as a Princess and climbed down as a Queen." Some claim that she was either asleep or having breakfast or even taking a photograph of the sunrise with an eagle hovering over her head. Another story goes that while she was there two waterbucks were fighting, with one fatally wounded. According to Kikuyu legend, when two waterbucks meet in combat and one dies, it signals the death of a great chief.

An official announcement of the King's death had been released in London, but it was several hours before Princess Elizabeth learned that she had been Queen since before dawn. By the time The Queen's aircraft touched down in London she was in the deepest mourning. Her arrival was captured in one of the most poignant photographs of her reign, as solitary, and looking touchingly vulnerable, she descended the steps of the Argonaut. She was met at the bottom by her Prime Minister, Winston Churchill, and the country's senior politicians.

At her Accession Council held in St James's Palace the following morning, The Queen read her formal Declaration of Sovereignty with controlled emotion and told her assembled Privy Counsellors: "My heart is too full for me to say more to you than that I shall always work as my father did." But to her cousin and close friend, Margaret Rhodes, she wrote of her agony at being thousands of miles away when her father died, adding: "It really was ghastly, the feeling that I was unable to help or comfort Mummy or Margaret, and that there was nothing that one could do at all."

Nine days after his death, King George VI was buried at Windsor to the thud of muffled drums. Winston Churchill's wreath bore the inscription "For Valour", the citation of the Victoria Cross, as a tribute to the leadership and courage the King had shown during the Second World War.

31 January 1952 King George VI *(right)*, Queen Elizabeth and Princess Margaret wave as Princess Elizabeth and The Duke of Edinburgh leave London Airport for Nairobi, Kenya, at the start of their Commonwealth tour.

7 February 1952 Queen Elizabeth II arrives at London Airport from Kenya, to be greeted by Winston Churchill, her first Prime Minister, after the sudden death of the King at Sandringham.

140 Extraordinary Years of Maldon Salt

Add a pinch of Maldon Salt to your celebrations

maldonsalt.com @maldonsalt

Photography: David Loftus

2 June 1953 Queen Elizabeth II, wearing St Edward's Crown and carrying the Sceptre with the Cross, and the Rod of Equity and Mercy, after the crowning ceremony at Westminster Abbey.

A QUEEN IS CROWNED

The day set for the Coronation was 2 June 1953. The nation was gripped with 'coronation fever', and the slightest fragment of information, true or untrue was avidly received.

In a broadcast to the nation, Winston Churchill forecast the dawn of a new Elizabethan age, declaring with a typical flourish: "Famous have been the reigns of our Queens. Some of the greatest periods in our history have unfolded under their sceptre." Newspaper headlines also predicted a spirit of revival and optimism centred on the young Queen – the nation's hope.

The Queen studied every part of the ancient ceremony, which would take place in Westminster Abbey. During the regular rehearsals in the Ballroom of Buckingham Palace, wearing a practice robe provided by Ede & Ravenscroft designed to replicate her Coronation Robes, she walked between posts and tapes marking the outline of her processional route.

The Queen appointed Prince Philip chairman of the Coronation Commission, and the ultimate success of the historic event owed much to his drive and energy. When she arrived at the Great West Door of Westminster Abbey, her Maids of Honour carefully unfolded the 21-feet-long train of the Robe of State. She turned to them and said: "Ready, girls. Set me off."

And so Her Majesty began her long walk up the Abbey's aisle towards the throne – and to take her place in the history of the monarchy. She took the Coronation oath in a clear unfaltering voice. After The Queen was crowned Prince Philip was the first, after the archbishops and bishops, to pay homage to her. He spoke with conviction, and never once would he falter in what he saw as his essential duty: supporting The Queen.

The Coronation was groundbreaking in its own right – the first ever to be televised, it was watched by 27 million people in the UK alone and millions more around the world.

After the ceremony the newly crowned Queen and her husband drove back to Buckingham Palace in the Gold State Coach to roar after roar of applause. In the Green Drawing Room and the Throne Room they posed for the eminent photographer, Cecil Beaton. He found The Queen "cool, smiling, sovereign of the situation, although looking weary from wearing the Crown for three hours".

"Yes", she remarked, "the Crown does get heavy". In the background, Prince Philip made wry jokes.

At 5.42pm The Queen and Prince Philip made the first of six balcony appearances. The last was at midnight in response to the "tumultuous loyalty" of the crowd, as the *Daily Telegraph* put it.

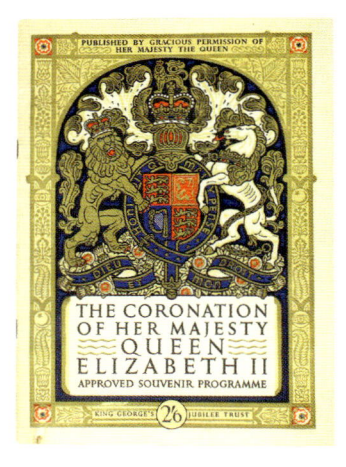

2 June 1953 The Queen, wearing the Imperial State Crown and her Coronation Robes, with Prince Philip in uniform as Admiral of the Fleet, in the Throne Room in Buckingham Palace, following the Coronation.

THE QUEEN'S REIGN

20 March 1995 The Queen presents Nelson Mandela, President of South Africa, with the Order of Merit, in Cape Town.

AROUND THE WORLD

Five months after the Coronation, The Queen and Prince Philip embarked on their longest-ever overseas tour. They were away for five-and-a-half months, a marathon of visits to Bermuda, Jamaica, Fiji, Tonga, New Zealand, Australia, the Cocos Islands, Ceylon (now Sri Lanka), Aden, Uganda, Malta and Gibraltar. The busy itinerary saw The Queen deliver more than 150 speeches, sometimes half a dozen in a single day.

Since that epic journey, there are few countries she has not visited as an ambassador for the interests of the United Kingdom. Although she represents a country whose imperial power has long gone, she is invariably greeted with instant recognition wherever she goes. In China, in 1986, she walked the Great Wall, and was addressed as "The English country female King".

The stability that The Queen represents in a deeply uncertain world is the object of a wider envy than is sometimes realised at home. Appreciating its virtue does not require an understanding of the intricacies of constitutional monarchy. It transcends politics, and even nationality. To admirers the world over Queen Elizabeth II is not just Queen of the United Kingdom, but The Queen.

THE COMMONWEALTH

As the Head of the Commonwealth, The Queen symbolises the unity and collaborative ethos underpinning this diverse group of nations which spans nearly a quarter of the globe. Not just a symbol of this free association of nations, Her Majesty has personally reinforced the links between the 54 member states through more than 200 royal tours, making her the most travelled monarch in history. In her Commonwealth Day Message for 2022, The Queen said it had given her "pleasure" to renew in her Platinum Jubilee year the promise she made in 1947, "that my life will always be devoted to your service". Her Majesty went on to hope that "the family of nations could draw strength" and inspiration from what we share "during these testing times".

8 March 2021 The Queen signs her annual Commonwealth Day Message in St George's Hall at Windsor Castle.

14 October 1986 The Queen and Prince Philip on the Great Wall of China at Badaling, 50 miles north-west of Beijing, on the third day of their State Visit to the country.

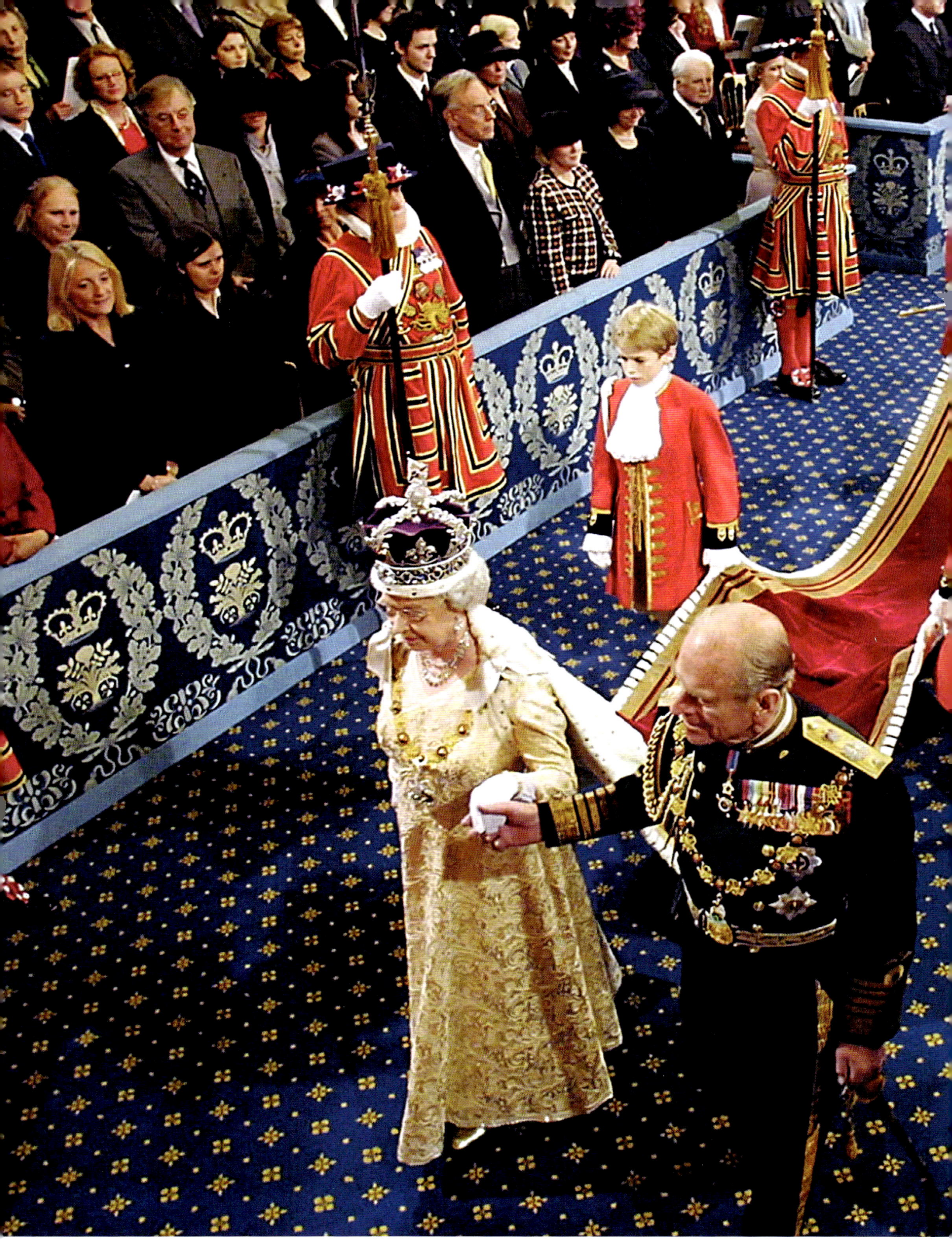

13 November 2002 The Queen, wearing the Imperial State Crown and escorted by Prince Philip, walks in procession through the Royal Gallery on her way to deliver her speech during the ceremonial State Opening of Parliament.

THE REIGN

Throughout a reign when society and its views have evolved rapidly, Her Majesty has remained self-sufficient, proficient in the business of monarchy and at ease in its routines: the official visits at home and overseas, receiving government ministers and ambassadors, grand ceremonial occasions, such as the State Opening of Parliament, and the visits of other Heads of State. More importantly, The Queen has to understand the State Papers, which follow her everywhere in their red boxes, even when she is on holiday. As Her Majesty says: "Luckily I'm a quick reader."

The Queen is extremely well informed in political matters. She has a special relationship with the prime minister, retaining the right to appoint and meet with them on a regular basis. To date 14 prime ministers, from Winston Churchill to Boris Johnson, have been received weekly in audience when Parliament is in session. They are carefully questioned, and sometimes challenged. As The Queen puts it when describing her relationship with her prime ministers: "Occasionally one can put one's point of view when perhaps they hadn't seen it from that angle."

As Titular Head of the Church of England, the Sovereign holds the title of "Defender of the Faith and Supreme Governor of the Church of England". Her personal faith has never wavered, and she has strong Christian beliefs, which were evident even before she became Queen.

In her first Christmas broadcast in 1952, six months before her Coronation, The Queen asked people to remember her at the time of her Coronation the following June: "Pray for me that God may give me wisdom and strength to carry out the solemn promises I shall be making and that I may faithfully serve Him and you all the days of my life."

Her Majesty regularly worships in the Royal Chapel of All Saints in Windsor Great Park; when she is at Sandringham she invariably attends St Mary Magdalene, situated on her Norfolk estate; and when in residence at Balmoral, she attends Crathie Kirk.

The Queen's reign has witnessed jet-engine travel, space exploration, multimedia, social revolution and global political upheaval. She has reigned through the emergence of new musical genres, from rock and roll to rave music, hip hop to Britpop, and more.

In this day and age, reference points for certainty are rare, but Her Majesty is without doubt one of them. In 1952 the then Princess found herself young, bereaved by the premature death of her father, and yet Head of State at a time when the country, still recovering from the effect of war, urgently needed to reshape its identity and its place in the world. That she rose to the occasion, ably assisted by Prince Philip, is a remarkable achievement.

23 December 2021 The Queen records her annual Christmas broadcast in the White Drawing Room in Windsor Castle.

There have, of course, been times of personal sadness. The death in 2002 of Princess Margaret, shortly followed by that of Queen Elizabeth The Queen Mother, were hard blows, but even worse was the loss of Prince Philip. And who will forget the image of The Queen sitting alone in St George's Chapel, Windsor, separated from her family. Eleven months after the Prince's funeral at Windsor, The Queen and her family attended the Service of Thanksgiving in Westminster Abbey to honour his memory.

In 2015, The Queen surpassed Queen Victoria as the United Kingdom's longest-reigning monarch. Characteristically, Her Majesty marked this milestone by working: opening the new Borders Railway in Scotland. There was no sense of triumph on the day. As one observer put it: "She made history, but with modesty and lack of ostentation that defines her; she gave a gentle passing wave and moved on."

It is a way of life The Queen took on at an early age and that she has no plans to relinquish, except by passing some of her more demanding tasks to other members of the Royal Family. Her Majesty is on record as saying that being Queen is "a job for life". And for many of us, life without her would be hard to imagine.

Clockwise from top left: **17 October 1980** Pope John Paul II exchanges gifts with The Queen and The Duke of Edinburgh during a visit to the Vatican in Rome, Italy.

5 June 1961 President John Kennedy of the United States of America *(right)* and First Lady Jacqueline Kennedy *(2nd left)* pictured with The Queen and The Duke of Edinburgh at Buckingham Palace.

24 May 2011 The Queen and The Duke of Edinburgh pose with President Barack Obama of the United States of America and First Lady Michelle Obama in the Music Room of Buckingham Palace ahead of a State Banquet.

19 October 2021 The Queen and Prime Minister Boris Johnson *(left)* meet attendees during a reception for delegates of the Global Investment Conference at Windsor Castle.

4 April 1955 Lady Churchill watches as Prime Minister Sir Winston Churchill, wearing his sash as a Knight of the Garter, welcomes The Queen and The Duke of Edinburgh to 10 Downing Street for dinner.

20 November 2007 To mark their Diamond Wedding anniversary, The Queen and Prince Philip revisited Broadlands in Hampshire, where 60 years previously they had spent part of their honeymoon.

PORTRAIT OF A MARRIAGE

Prince Philip was the only man in the world who treated The Queen as though she was just another person. In public and in private he was The Queen's compass and confidante, often advising on her speeches and engagements.

Those who knew them well say there was a deep bond of love and affection between them. They had much to say to each other, and more importantly, they listened to each other. They both had a strong sense of humour sharpened over the years by an appreciation of the ridiculous. They made each other laugh. Wedding anniversaries were marked by the arrival of an enormous bouquet, presented to The Queen by her husband after breakfast. The flowers were never forgotten, even if he was on the other side of the world. At home she deferred to him, often telling friends: "I'll see what Philip thinks."

Prince Philip readily admitted that he had always done his own thing, but at the same time he resolutely maintained that supporting and protecting The Queen "without getting in the way" was his paramount duty. The media had, on occasions, assumed that he had experienced problems with equating the role of husband and subject, but there was no real evidence to suggest that he found this difficult. As the years and anniversaries came and went, the magnetism was still there. They were well matched. A good team.

15 April 2003 The Queen and Prince Philip enjoy the spectacle, as a swarm of bees cause concern prior to The Queen's Company Review at Windsor Castle.

At the time of their Golden Wedding anniversary in 1997, Prince Philip said of The Queen: "The main lesson we have learned is that tolerance is the one essential ingredient of any happy marriage. It might not be quite so important when things are going well, but it is absolutely vital when the going gets difficult. The Queen has the quality of tolerance in abundance." In her own speech to mark this anniversary, The Queen memorably said of Prince Philip: "He is someone who doesn't take easily to compliments, but he has, quite simply, been my strength and stay all these years." ◆

3 November 2017
The Official Platinum
Wedding Portrait of
The Queen and Prince Philip.

28 July 1977 The Queen is cheered on by a huge crowd at Butterley Hall, near Chesterfield, during her Silver Jubilee tour.

JUBILEES PAST & PRESENT

Jubilees celebrate the life and reign of a monarch, and are significant historical events which are celebrated around the world.

Princess Elizabeth was only nine years old when she first experienced official events to mark a Jubilee, attending the Service of Thanksgiving at St Paul's Cathedral that celebrated the Silver Jubilee of her paternal grandparents, King George V and Queen Mary, in 1935.

That day the Princess was closer to the throne than she or anyone else could have ever imagined. The King had only seven months to live, and she was three months short of her tenth birthday when she became heir presumptive on the accession of her father, King George VI, second in line to the throne, following the unexpected abdication of his elder brother, King Edward VIII.

But that was all in the future, and when King George and Queen Mary appeared on the Buckingham Palace balcony they were cheered by a vast crowd. The King was astonished by the warmth of his reception and said: "I am beginning to think they must really like me for myself."

He was not only King of the United Kingdom and the British dominions overseas, but also Emperor of India, and his Jubilee celebrations were marked by reference to these imperial connections. Subsequent Jubilees – the Silver, Golden, Diamond and now Platinum Jubilees of his granddaughter – have reflected the changing relationships between nations, including the vibrant growth of the Commonwealth during the seven decades of Queen Elizabeth II's reign.

In the summer of 1977, Britain erupted into a riot of red, white and blue. The Queen's Silver Jubilee, marking 25 years of her reign, was a runaway success, and the principal participant said that she was "floored" by the spontaneous explosion of excitement and displays of affection. The Queen's walkabouts resembled a coronation by popular acclaim, but for Her Majesty, the celebrations gave focus to her reign, and to the life she had dedicated to service and duty.

The Golden and Diamond Jubilees were similar in their measure of loyalty and affection. The Queen called her Golden Jubilee "a pretty remarkable 50 years by any standards", adding, "I think we can look back with measured pride on the history of the last 50 years". And Her Majesty summed up her affection for the people of Britain and the Commonwealth, by expressing her "gratitude, respect, and pride".

The compliment was enthusiastically returned by huge crowds both at home and overseas. The Queen's Diamond Jubilee was a commensurate triumph. Her Majesty said it had been "a humbling" experience, which had "touched her deeply". ✦

5 June 2012 Thousands of revellers watch the ceremonial flypast by the RAF from around the Queen Victoria Memorial at Buckingham Palace during the Diamond Jubilee celebrations.

SEVEN DECADES OF ROYAL STYLE

Discover the fashion of The Queen's reign.

| 1950s | 1960s | 1970s | 1980s | 1990s | 2000s | 2010s |

6 May 1960 Worn by The Queen for the marriage of Princess Margaret to Antony Armstrong-Jones, at Westminster Abbey, this ensemble was designed by Norman Hartnell, who was also responsible for Princess Margaret's wedding dress and the outfits worn by the principal female members of the Royal Family attending the service. Cecil Beaton, the official photographer of the wedding, described his portrait of The Queen taken on this occasion: "The Queen was enormously appealing to me. Her dress was quite wonderfully romantic – with a skirt of stiff folds – and everything of a kingfisher brilliance."

SEVEN DECADES OF ROYAL STYLE

1956 The Queen, in a black evening gown and tiara, greets film star Marilyn Monroe at the Royal premiere of *The Battle of the River Plate*.

2009 The Queen, wearing a long, sparkling black gown, meets American singer Lady Gaga following the Royal Variety Performance in Blackpool.

The Queen has a keen awareness of the power of what she wears. It is all about visibility; making a woman of five feet four inches instantly recognisable. Therefore, she favours strong colours. Beige, for instance, is a non-starter, because, as she once remarked, "Nobody would know who I am." The Queen's hats must neither shadow her face, nor fly off in a breeze. Her Majesty once claimed: "I've never lost a hat yet."

The Queen's skirt hems are believed to be weighted, to keep them in place when getting out of a car. She is adept at what she calls "a big dressing" – when hosting a State Banquet, for instance. And the story is told that when she was younger, she could put on a tiara while running downstairs.

On visits overseas, The Queen has always been adamant that her outfits should pay homage to the host country, either by use of colour or by design, and that they should send specific messages. For example, on her landmark visit to the Republic of Ireland in 2011 she wore emerald green, the colour most closely associated with Ireland. The gold dress The Queen wore in 2012 for the Diamond Jubilee concert in front of Buckingham Palace was influenced by the golden figure representing Victory on top of the Queen Victoria Memorial. The white, jewel-studded outfit worn for the Thames River Pageant in the same year was inspired by the magnificent gowns favoured by Elizabeth I, celebrated in history as a superb power-dresser. The dress was designed by Angela Kelly, The Queen's Personal Adviser and Dresser, and took more than a year to make. According to Ms Kelly, the white was chosen to contrast with the strong reds of the royal barge's upholstery.

When she was a young Queen, and before that as Princess Elizabeth, Norman Hartnell, the maestro of glamorous evening gowns created the full-skirted, fairy-tale ball gowns, that remain among the finest evening dresses in Her Majesty's wardrobe. Hartnell's triumph was The Queen's splendid Coronation Dress. She insisted that its design included an emblem for every part of the United Kingdom and the other Commonwealth countries. But it was Hardy Amies who shone when it came to designing The Queen's day clothes. His talent for tailoring and deceptive simplicity eased Her Majesty into the sharper silhouettes of the 1960s, 1970s and 1980s. And in this, her Platinum Jubilee year, she will look as she always has done: every inch a Queen. ✦

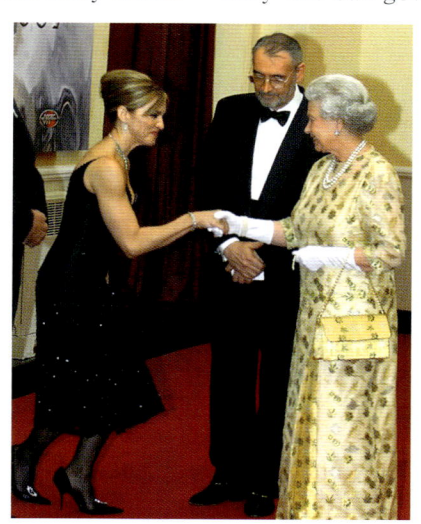

2002 The Queen, wearing a stunning gold floral print gown, meets pop queen Madonna at the world premiere of the James Bond film *Die Another Day*, at the Royal Albert Hall in London.

1 July 1969 For the Investiture of Prince Charles as Prince of Wales at Caernarfon Castle, The Queen wore an ensemble of pale primrose yellow comprising a silk crepe long-sleeved coat and matching tunic, both decorated with pearl and bugle bead embroidery. A panel of silk with lines of embroidery is attached to the crown of the hat, covering the back of the head to the nape of the neck. The hat appears to have been inspired by Tudor prototypes and was a style repeated on several occasions in different colours and materials.

SEVEN DECADES OF ROYAL STYLE

Top: **11 June 2016** The Queen, in a neon-green Stewart Parvin coat and dress, with a matching Rachel Trevor-Morgan hat, on the balcony of Buckingham Palace, joined by Prince Philip, The Duke and Duchess of Cambridge, Prince George and Princess Charlotte, after the Trooping the Colour parade that marked Her Majesty's Official 90th Birthday.

Above: **4 June 2012** The Queen, resplendent in a shimmering gold dress, accessorised with a string of pearls and matching earrings, handbag and mink-coloured gloves, meets Sir Paul McCartney, Sir Tom Jones, Dame Shirley Bassey, Sir Cliff Richard and Sir Elton John at the Diamond Jubilee Concert at Buckingham Palace.

3 June 2012 The Queen, wearing a sparkling white frill-edged Angela Kelly coat and dress with matching hat, on Chelsea Pier during the Diamond Jubilee River Pageant.

6 July 2017 The Queen, wearing a peachy pink Stewart Parvin coat with a Rachel Trevor-Morgan flat-crowned straw hat of the same colour embellished with multi-looped side bows and silk blooms, during a visit to the new Highland Spring factory building in Blackford, Perthshire.

SEVEN DECADES OF ROYAL STYLE

Above: **30 July 1966** The Queen chose a striking warm-yellow coat and matching hat for *that* World Cup Final at Wembley Stadium.

11 December 1962 The Queen, in a white silk faille gown, shakes hands with actor Peter O'Toole before the world charity premiere of the film *Lawrence of Arabia* in London.

Left: **14 November 2006** The Queen, in a shimmering lilac floral print gown and classic long white gloves, meets actor Daniel Craig at the world premiere for the James Bond film *Casino Royale* in London.

10 October 2014 The Queen, wearing a peach dress and pearls, presents actress Angelina Jolie with the Insignia of an Honorary Dame Commander of the Most Distinguished Order of St Michael and St George, in the 1844 Room at Buckingham Palace.

27 October 1958 The Queen, wearing a strapped swirl-effect evening gown and tiara, meets Frank Sinatra at the premiere of Danny Kaye's film *Me and the Colonel* at London's Empire Cinema.

TRUEFITT & HILL

EST. 1805 · ST. JAMES'S · LONDON

Congratulations on the occasion of the Platinum Jubilee to HM The Queen!

GROOMING MEN FOR GREATNESS SINCE 1805

THE PLATINUM QUEEN

The Crown Jewels form part of the Royal Collection, and are also a part of our national heritage and still regularly used by The Queen. Her Majesty also has an entirely separate personal collection of jewellery. Let's take a closer look at some of the finest examples of diamond jewels in the world ...

On this page: The Diamond Diadem, worn by The Queen on her journey to and from the State Opening of Parliament since the first year of her reign. It is set with 1,333 brilliant-cut diamonds, including a four-carat pale yellow brilliant. It consists of a band with two rows of pearls either side of a row of diamonds, above which are diamonds set in the form of a rose, a thistle and two shamrocks – the national emblems of England, Scotland and Ireland.

THE PLATINUM QUEEN

The Queen's jewels are unique in their remarkable historic provenance. Mainly dating from the 19th and 20th centuries, they include historic heirloom jewels inherited from Her Majesty's predecessors together with pieces that have been presented to her during her reign and are often of great personal significance. Queen Victoria's diamond collet necklace, made by R. & S. Garrard in 1858, was worn by The Queen at her Coronation on 2 June 1953, just as it had been by Queen Alexandra, Queen Mary and Queen Elizabeth at their own coronations.

In 1947, the then Princess Elizabeth received a number of significant jewels on her 21st birthday. These included a necklace comprising 21 brilliant diamonds set in platinum, presented by the Government of the Union of South Africa. On the occasion of Princess Elizabeth's marriage to Prince Philip on 23 November 1947, her grandmother, Queen Mary, presented her with a number of gifts, including the Girls of Great Britain and Ireland Tiara, which had originally been a wedding gift to the Duchess of York (later Queen Mary). Created in the fashionable garland style, the tiara has become one of the most recognisable during The Queen's reign, particularly as it was worn for her Accession portraits and to this day is depicted in the profile portraits of Her Majesty on our coinage and banknotes.

The Queen has inherited some spectacular and famous stones, including the jewels made from the magnificent Cullinan diamond. Discovered at the Premier Mine in Pretoria in 1905, the Cullinan diamond is the largest uncut diamond ever found and was presented to King Edward VII in 1907 as a token of loyalty by the Transvaal Government. The diamond was cleaved into nine principal numbered stones, including Cullinan III and IV, which The Queen has regularly worn as a brooch throughout her reign.

Distinct from The Queen's 'wearing' jewellery are the Crown Jewels, a symbol of monarchy for the British people and part of their national heritage. With one or two notable exceptions, the Regalia, as they are collectively known, date from the coronation of Charles II in 1661.

The Imperial State Crown is perhaps the most recognisable crown, and it was altered for the Coronation of Queen Elizabeth II in 1953. Apart from their great historical value, the Crown Jewels also contain some notable gems, including the First and Second Stars of Africa, the two largest stones from the Cullinan Diamond, the Koh-i-Nûr diamonds, St Edward's Sapphire, Queen Elizabeth's pearls, the Black Prince's Ruby and the Stuart Sapphire.

The Queen does not wear her jewels for personal vanity, displaying them only as accoutrements of majesty when the occasion demands, for State Banquets, Royal Tours and the State Opening of Parliament. ✦

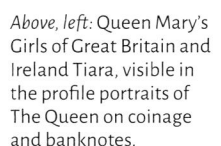

Above, left: Queen Mary's Girls of Great Britain and Ireland Tiara, visible in the profile portraits of The Queen on coinage and banknotes.

Top: The Cullinan V Brooch (originally worn by Queen Mary for the Delhi Durbar in 1911, marking King George V's succession as King Emperor of India). The Queen inherited the brooch in 1953 from her grandmother.

Middle: The Cullinan III and IV Brooch, worn by The Queen for the Service of Thanksgiving for Her Majesty's Diamond Jubilee, at St Paul's Cathedral, on 5 June 2012.

Above, right: The diamond necklace worn by The Queen at the Coronation in 1953. The central 22.48 carat diamond pendant is known as the Lahore Diamond.

The Queen wearing the Girls of Great Britain and Ireland Tiara, and two pieces designed by Prince Albert for Queen Victoria: the Crown Ruby Necklace and accompanying Brooch.

THE PLATINUM QUEEN

THE CROWN JEWELS

Powerful symbols of Majesty.

The British Crown Jewels are a world-famous and unique collection of sacred and ceremonial regalia worn by our kings and queens since the 16th century. The regalia is housed in the Tower of London, or, to give this history-rich building its official title, "Her Majesty's Royal Palace and Fortress of the Tower of London".

The Crown Jewels are kept in the Jewel House, a secure vault within the precincts of the Tower, which was reopened by The Queen in 1994. The priceless gems, each one steeped in history, sit glittering and glistening on blue velvet behind bombproof glass, covered by a hundred hidden CCTV cameras, and guarded by a 22-man detachment of soldiers and 88 Yeoman Warders who can close the Jewel House's six-inch-thick two-ton steel doors in seconds. This is all in stark contrast to the protection the jewels received during the Second World War when they were buried within the grounds of Windsor Castle, with some of the most significant diamonds hidden in a large biscuit tin. More than 30 million people have been recorded as seeing the jewels in their present setting, and they are probably the most visited treasures in the United Kingdom, perhaps in the world.

At the heart of the collection is the Coronation Regalia, a group of precious and highly symbolic objects used to crown the Sovereign since the coronation of Charles II in 1661, following the Restoration of the Monarchy. Spiritually, St Edward's Crown is the most important of all the crowns on display, and it is only used at the moment of crowning itself. The Sovereign's orb symbolises the Christian world, with its cross mounted on a globe, while the Sovereign's Sceptre features in the investiture sequence of the Coronation. The Imperial State Crown is worn by the newly crowned Sovereign when returning to Buckingham Palace from Westminster Abbey. It is also customarily worn for the State Opening of Parliament. These treasures can all be viewed in the Jewel House, with the exception of the Diamond Diadem, worn by The Queen on the journey to her Coronation from Buckingham Palace to Westminster Abbey. ✦

Top: St Edward's Crown, composed of a solid gold frame set with semi-precious stones, including rubies, amethysts, sapphires, garnet, topazes and tourmalines. The Crown has a velvet cap with an ermine band.

Above: The Sovereign's Orb is formed of a hollow gold sphere, mounted with clusters of emeralds, rubies and sapphires surrounded by rose-cut diamonds and single rows of pearls. The cross is set with with rose-cut diamonds, with a sapphire and an emerald on each side, and with pearls at the angles and at the end of each arm.

The Imperial State Crown, worn by The Queen at the State Opening of Parliament, and also by the newly crowned Sovereign when returning to Buckingham Palace from Westminster Abbey.

THE QUEEN'S GREEN CANOPY

THE QUEEN'S GREEN CANOPY

THE PLATINUM JUBILEE 2022

PLANT A TREE FOR THE JUBILEE

October 2021 – December 2022

The Queen's Green Canopy is a unique tree-planting initiative created to mark Her Majesty's Platinum Jubilee which invites people from across the United Kingdom to "Plant a Tree for the Jubilee".

The Queen has planted many trees during her reign, but now she is the figurehead of a unique tree-planting campaign: "The Queen's Green Canopy". Created to celebrate Her Majesty's Platinum Jubilee, it invites people from across the United Kingdom to plant a Jubilee tree. Individuals, groups, villages, cities, counties and corporate bodies are being encouraged to join in, wield their spades and enhance the environment in this very special year.

The aim is to encourage everyone to get involved by planting trees from autumn 2021 to the end of the Jubilee year. The result will be both spectacular and sustainable: a legacy to honour The Queen's leadership of the nation over seven decades, and one that will benefit future generations, including a trial training programme for unemployed young people aged between 16 and 24 to learn how to plant, protect and manage trees.

As well as inviting the planting of new trees, the initiative will dedicate a network of 70 unique and irreplaceable Ancient Woodlands across the United Kingdom, and help identify 70 Ancient Trees to celebrate Her Majesty's service to the nation.

The Queen and The Prince of Wales planted the first Jubilee tree in the grounds of Windsor Castle to mark the launch of the Canopy, followed by another tree at Balmoral Castle. Other members of the Royal Family have also planted Jubilee trees at home and abroad.

Ahead of the Platinum Jubilee celebrations in June, Her Majesty has offered her deep gratitude to all involved: "As planting season draws to a close, I send my sincere thanks to everyone across the country who has planted a tree to celebrate my Platinum Jubilee.

"I am deeply touched that so many community groups, schools, families and individuals have made their own unique contributions to the Green Canopy initiative.

"I hope your Jubilee trees flourish and grow for many years to come, for future generations to enjoy."

So far, since autumn 2021, a remarkable *one million* trees have now been successfully planted as part of The Queen's initiative. Well done, everyone! ✦

1 October 2021 The Queen and The Prince of Wales planted a copper beech tree at Balmoral Castle's historic cricket pavilion, to mark the start of the campaign to "Plant a Tree for the Jubilee".

THE QUEEN'S GREEN CANOPY

THE QUEEN'S GREEN CANOPY
THE PLATINUM JUBILEE 2022

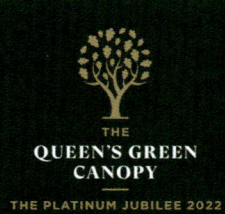

How to get involved

1. PLAN

Learn about tree planting season, where to plant, and how to secure a tree. You will need to consider the time of year. Experts recommend planting trees between October and March, when they are dormant and less likely to be damaged during planting. The summer months are a good time to plan your project, ready for planting during the autumn. It is important to think about the size and spread of the trees and how you will use the site as the trees grow. There are many different varieties of trees, all of which have different characteristics, purposes and needs (soil, water, nutrients). Most trees can grow in a range of conditions, though some will prefer particular soil types.

2. PLANT

Having completed the important planning stage, where you learnt when and where to plant, and how to secure a healthy tree, the jubilant moment of planting your tree has arrived. Begin by preparing the surrounding ground. A happy tree will have plenty of light and water, so remove any overgrown weeds, especially grass which will compete with the tree for light, nutrients and water. While there are various methods to plant a tree, on our website at **queensgreencanopy.org** we have outlined the pit planting method, which is suitable for most types of soil, alongside advice on planting a sapling and fitting a spiral or tree guard to protect it.

3. PROTECT

Learn how you can give your tree the best chance of flourishing. In their first few years, there are several steps you can take to ensure the trees you have planted have the best chance of thriving. To help with this, it may be beneficial to appoint tree stewards, or someone responsible for taking care of the tree. The needs of trees will vary as they grow, from watering, weeding, adding mulch, and simply keeping a close eye on your tree.

For further information, visit queensgreencanopy.org

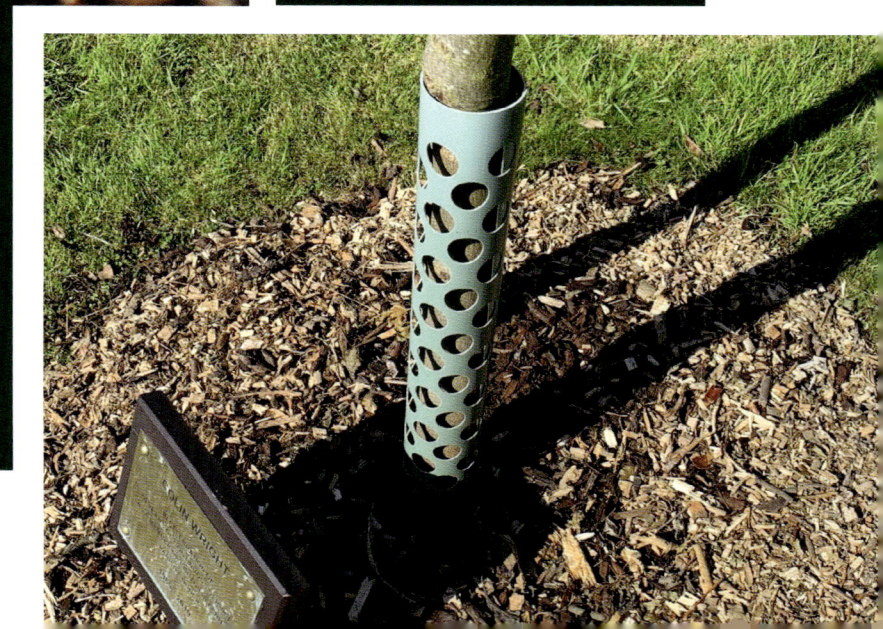

Bloomberg is proud to celebrate the Queen's Platinum Jubilee

and support diverse, vibrant and sustainable communities across the UK.

Bloomberg | Bloomberg Philanthropies

Visual by PicturePlane for Heatherwick Studio

THE QUEEN'S GREEN CANOPY

THE QUEEN'S GREEN CANOPY

THE PLATINUM JUBILEE 2022

TREE OF TREES

June, Buckingham Palace

A spectacular 21-metre "Tree of Trees" sculpture featuring 350 British native trees will be created outside Buckingham Palace as an exciting centrepiece of The Queen's Platinum Jubilee weekend celebrations in June.

Designed by British architect Thomas Heatherwick, the sculpture reflects the joyful Jubilee tree planting which has swept the nation as part of The Queen's Green Canopy (QGC), inspiring over a million trees to be planted during its first season, from October to March.

The sculpture seeks to put the importance of trees and nature at the heart of this historic milestone to celebrate Her Majesty, who has planted more than 1,500 trees all over the world during the course of her 70-year reign.

The 350 trees will be set in recycled aluminium pots embossed with Her Majesty's cypher. After the Jubilee weekend, the trees will be given to selected community groups and organisations to celebrate their work and inspire the next generation of tree planters across the nation. The trees will be carefully stored during the summer ahead of distribution at the start of the planting season in October. Further details on the selection process will be announced in due course.

The Queen's Green Canopy is working to help green our cities, renew the countryside and bring communities together. Working with partners, a key element of the QGC includes a programme to support urban greening projects in areas of high socioeconomic deprivation and low canopy cover. With trees at the heart of his urban designs, Thomas Heatherwick's work reflects this theme, with a mission to find innovative and sustainable ways to integrate trees into cities and communities. ✦

Congratulations Your Majesty on 70 Glorious Years

LOLA ROSE

LONDON

DISCOVER A WORLD OF TIMELESS ELEGANCE

A GALLOP THROUGH HISTORY

Thursday 12 May – Sunday 15 May, Windsor

The ancient walls of Windsor Castle formed the backdrop to one of the most spectacular events of Her Majesty's Platinum Jubilee celebrations. A 90-minute piece of spell-binding theatre, "A Gallop Through History" time-travelled from the reign of Elizabeth I – played by Dame Helen Mirren – through to the Coronation of Her Majesty The Queen. Other performers included Dame Joan Collins, Damian Lewis OBE, Sir Mo Farah, Dame Maureen Lipman, and Katherine Jenkins OBE. It was light-hearted and respectful, and, above all, a tribute to The Queen.

The programme was broadcast live on ITV, hosted by broadcaster Alan Titchmarsh MBE and actor Tom Cruise, and featured music by a 75-piece orchestra. The show narrated five centuries of kings and queens, as well as significant events in our island's story, and featured more than 1,000 performers and 500 horses. The crowd was entertained with pomp and pageantry, military displays from the Commonwealth, Europe and our own armed forces, equestrianism and dancing. The occasion was hosted by the Royal Windsor Horse Show. ✦